Charmides by Plato

Translated by Benjamin Jowett

For someone whose influence has been so profound on Western thinking remarkably little is known of the Greek philosopher and thinker Plato.

Due to the means and social status of his family Plato was most probably educated by some of Athens' finest teachers. The curriculum would have been rich and varied and include the doctrines of Cratylus and Pythagoras as well as Parmenides.

Two major events shaped Plato's life whilst he was a young man. The first was a meeting with the great philosopher Socrates. Socrates's methods of debate impressed Plato and he soon became a devoted follower. From here would flow Plato's career as one of the finest minds civilization has produced.

Major event number two was the on-going rivalry between Athens and Sparta which erupted into the Peloponnesian War. This was, in fact, several 'stop-start' wars fought during the period 431–404 BCE. Plato served in the cause of Athens and its Allies between 409 and 404 B.C.E. The comprehensive defeat of Athens by Sparta ended the Athenian democracy, although after a brief oligarchy it was restored.

Plato traveled for a dozen years throughout the Mediterranean, studying mathematics with the Pythagoreans in Italy, as well as geometry, geology, astronomy and religion in Egypt. It was during this time that Plato began his writings, a remarkable number of which survive to this day.

The writings themselves are usually classified into three distinct periods although there is some uncertainty as to the exact order in which they were written.

Having now returned to Athens Plato embarked upon an extraordinary undertaking. In around 385 B.C.E., he established a school of learning, known as the Academy. The extensive curriculum included astronomy, biology, mathematics, political theory and philosophy. Plato hoped that those who studied there would be future leaders who would be better equipped thorough its teachings to understand how to build a better government. Plato would preside over its teachings until his death in Athens around 348 B.C.E.

Index of Contents

The subject of the Charmides is Temperance or (Greek), a peculiarly Greek notion, which may also be rendered Moderation (Compare Cic. Tusc. '(Greek), quam soleo equidem tum temperantiam, tum moderationem appellare, nonnunquam etiam modestiam.'), Modesty, Discretion, Wisdom, without completely exhausting by all these terms the various associations of the word. It may be described as 'mens sana in corpore sano,' the harmony or due proportion of the higher and lower elements of human nature which 'makes a man his own master,' according to the definition of the Republic. In the accompanying translation the word has been rendered in different places either Temperance or Wisdom, as the connection seemed to require: for in the philosophy of Plato (Greek) still retains an intellectual element (as Socrates is also said to have identified (Greek) with (Greek): Xen. Mem.) and is not yet relegated to the sphere of moral virtue, as in the Nicomachean Ethics of Aristotle.

The beautiful youth, Charmides, who is also the most temperate of human beings, is asked by Socrates, 'What is Temperance?' He answers characteristically, 'Quietness.' 'But Temperance is a fine and noble thing; and quietness in many or most cases is not so fine a thing as quickness.' He tries again and says that temperance is modesty. But this again is set aside by a sophistical application of Homer: for temperance is good as well as noble, and Homer has declared that 'modesty is not good for a needy man.' Once more Charmides makes the attempt. This time he gives a definition which he has heard, and of which Socrates conjectures that Critias must be the author: 'Temperance is doing one's own business.' But the artisan who makes another man's shoes may be temperate, and yet he is not doing his own business; and temperance defined thus would be opposed to the division of labour which exists in every temperate or well-ordered state. How is this riddle to be explained?

Critias, who takes the place of Charmides, distinguishes in his answer between 'making' and 'doing,' and with the help of a misapplied quotation from Hesiod assigns to the words 'doing' and 'work' an exclusively good sense: Temperance is doing one's own business;— is doing good.

Still an element of knowledge is wanting which Critias is readily induced to admit at the suggestion of Socrates; and, in the spirit of Socrates and of Greek life generally, proposes as a fifth definition, Temperance is self-knowledge. But all sciences have a subject: number is the subject of arithmetic, health of medicine—what is the subject of temperance or wisdom? The answer is that Temperance is the knowledge of what a man knows and of what he does not know. But this is contrary to analogy; there is no vision of vision, but only of visible things; no love of loves, but only of beautiful things; how then can there be a knowledge of knowledge? That which is older, heavier, lighter, is older, heavier, and lighter than something else, not than itself, and this seems to be true of all relative notions—the object of relation is outside of them; at any rate they can only have relation to themselves in the form of that object. Whether there are any such cases of reflex relation or not, and whether that sort of knowledge which we term Temperance is of this reflex nature, has yet to be determined by the great metaphysician. But even if knowledge can know itself, how does the knowledge of what we know imply the knowledge of what we do not know? Besides, knowledge is an abstraction only, and will not inform us of any particular subject, such as medicine, building, and the like. It may tell us that we or other men know something, but can never tell us what we know.

Admitting that there is a knowledge of what we know and of what we do not know, which would supply a rule and measure of all things, still there would be no good in this; and the knowledge which temperance gives must be of a kind which will do us good; for temperance is a good. But this universal knowledge does not tend to our happiness and good: the only kind of knowledge which brings happiness is the knowledge of good and evil. To this Critias replies that the science or knowledge of good and evil, and all the other sciences, are regulated by the higher science or knowledge of knowledge. Socrates replies by again dividing the abstract from the concrete, and asks how this knowledge conduces to happiness in the same definite way in which medicine conduces to health.

And now, after making all these concessions, which are really inadmissible, we are still as far as ever from ascertaining the nature of temperance, which Charmides has already discovered, and had therefore better rest in the knowledge that the more temperate he is the happier he will be, and not trouble himself with the speculations of Socrates.

In this Dialogue may be noted (1) The Greek ideal of beauty and goodness, the vision of the fair soul in the fair body, realised in the beautiful Charmides; (2) The true conception of medicine as a science of the whole as well as the parts, and of the mind as well as the body, which is playfully intimated in the story of the Thracian; (3) The tendency of the age to verbal distinctions, which here, as in the Protagoras and Cratylus, are ascribed to the ingenuity of Prodicus; and to interpretations or rather parodies of Homer or Hesiod, which are eminently characteristic of Plato and his contemporaries; (4) The germ of an ethical principle contained in the notion that temperance is 'doing one's own business,' which in the Republic (such is the shifting character of the Platonic philosophy) is given as the definition, not of temperance, but of justice; (5) The impatience which is exhibited by Socrates of any definition of temperance in which an element of science or knowledge is not included; (6) The beginning of metaphysics and logic implied in the two questions: whether there can be a science of science, and whether the knowledge of what you know is the same as the knowledge of what you do not know; and also in the distinction between 'what you know' and 'that you know,' (Greek;) here too is the first conception of an absolute self-determined science (the claims of which, however, are disputed by Socrates, who asks cui bono?) as well as the first suggestion of the difficulty of the abstract and concrete, and one of the earliest anticipations of the relation of subject and object, and of the subjective element in knowledge—a 'rich banquet' of metaphysical questions in which we 'taste of many things.' (7) And still the mind of Plato, having snatched for a moment at these shadows of the future, quickly rejects them: thus early has he reached the conclusion that there can be no science which is a 'science of nothing' (Parmen.). (8) The conception of a science of good and evil also first occurs here, an anticipation of the Philebus and Republic as well as of moral philosophy in later ages.

The dramatic interest of the Dialogue chiefly centres in the youth Charmides, with whom Socrates talks in the kindly spirit of an elder. His childlike simplicity and ingenuousness are contrasted with the dialectical and rhetorical arts of Critias, who is the grown-up man of the world, having a tincture of philosophy. No hint is given, either here or in the Timaeus, of the infamy which attaches to the name of the latter in Athenian history. He is simply a cultivated person who, like his kinsman Plato, is ennobled by the connection of his family with Solon (Tim.), and had been the follower, if not the disciple, both of Socrates and of the Sophists. In the argument he is not unfair, if allowance is made for a slight rhetorical tendency, and for a natural desire to save his reputation with the company; he is sometimes nearer the truth than Socrates. Nothing in his language or behaviour is unbecoming the guardian of the beautiful Charmides. His love of reputation is characteristically Greek, and contrasts with the humility of Socrates. Nor in Charmides himself do we find any resemblance to the Charmides of history, except, perhaps, the modest and retiring nature which, according to Xenophon, at one time of his life prevented him from speaking in the Assembly (Mem.); and we are surprised to hear that, like Critias, he afterwards became one of the thirty tyrants. In the Dialogue he is a pattern of virtue, and is therefore in no need of the charm which Socrates is unable to apply. With youthful naivete, keeping his secret and entering into the spirit of Socrates, he enjoys the detection of his elder and guardian Critias, who is easily seen to be the author of the definition which he has so great an interest in maintaining. The preceding definition, 'Temperance is doing one's own business,' is assumed to have been borrowed by Charmides from another; and when the enquiry becomes more abstract he is superseded by Critias (Theaet.; Euthyd.). Socrates preserves his accustomed irony to the end; he is in the neighbourhood of several great truths, which he views in various lights, but always either by bringing them to the test of common sense, or by demanding too great exactness in the use of words, turns aside from them and comes at last to no conclusion.

The definitions of temperance proceed in regular order from the popular to the philosophical. The first two are simple enough and partially true, like the first thoughts of an intelligent youth; the third, which is a real contribution to ethical philosophy, is perverted by the ingenuity of Socrates, and hardly rescued by an equal perversion on the part of Critias. The remaining definitions have a higher aim, which is to introduce the element of knowledge, and at last to unite good and truth in a single science. But the time has not yet arrived for the realization of this vision of metaphysical philosophy; and such a science when brought nearer to us in the Philebus and the Republic will not be called by the name of (Greek). Hence we see with surprise that Plato, who in his other writings identifies good and knowledge, here opposes them, and asks, almost in the spirit of Aristotle, how can there be a knowledge of knowledge, and even if attainable, how can such a knowledge be of any use?

The difficulty of the Charmides arises chiefly from the two senses of the word (Greek), or temperance. From the ethical notion of temperance, which is variously defined to be quietness, modesty, doing our own business, the doing of good actions, the dialogue passes onto the intellectual conception of (Greek), which is declared also to be the science of self-knowledge, or of the knowledge of what we know and do not know, or of the knowledge of good and evil. The dialogue represents a stage in the history of philosophy in which knowledge and action were not yet distinguished. Hence the confusion between them, and the easy transition from one to the other. The definitions which are offered are all rejected, but it is to be observed that they all tend to throw a light on the nature of temperance, and that, unlike the distinction of Critias between (Greek), none of them are merely verbal quibbles, it is implied that this question, although it has not yet received a solution in theory, has been already answered by Charmides himself, who has learned to practise the virtue of self-knowledge which philosophers are vainly trying to define in words. In a similar spirit we might say to a young man who is disturbed by theological difficulties, 'Do not trouble yourself about such matters, but only lead a good life;' and yet in either case it is not to be denied that right ideas of truth may contribute greatly to the improvement of character.

The reasons why the Charmides, Lysis, Laches have been placed together and first in the series of Platonic dialogues, are: (i) Their shortness and simplicity. The Charmides and the Lysis, if not the Laches, are of the same 'quality' as the Phaedrus and Symposium: and it is probable, though far from certain, that the slighter effort preceded the greater one. (ii) Their eristic, or rather Socratic character; they belong to the class called dialogues of search (Greek), which have no conclusion. (iii) The absence in them of certain favourite notions of Plato, such as the doctrine of recollection and of the Platonic ideas; the questions, whether virtue can be taught; whether the virtues are one or many. (iv) They have a want of depth, when compared with the dialogues of the middle and later period; and a youthful beauty and grace which is wanting in the later ones. (v) Their resemblance to one another; in all the three boyhood has a great part. These reasons have various degrees of weight in determining their place in the catalogue of the Platonic writings, though they are not conclusive. No arrangement of the Platonic dialogues can be strictly chronological. The order which has been adopted is intended mainly for the convenience of the reader; at the same time, indications of the date supplied either by Plato himself or allusions found in the dialogues have not been lost sight of. Much may be said about this subject, but the results can only be probable; there are no materials which would enable us to attain to anything like certainty.

The relations of knowledge and virtue are again brought forward in the companion dialogues of the Lysis and Laches; and also in the Protagoras and Euthydemus. The opposition of abstract and particular knowledge in this dialogue may be compared with a similar opposition of ideas and phenomena which occurs in the Prologues to the Parmenides, but seems rather to belong to a later stage of the philosophy of Plato.

CHARMIDES, OR TEMPERANCE

PERSONS OF THE DIALOGUE:
Socrates, who is the narrator,
Charmides,
Chaerephon,
Critias.

SCENE: The Palaestra of Taureas, which is near the Porch of the King Archon.

Yesterday evening I returned from the army at Potidaea, and having been a good while away, I thought that I should like to go and look at my old haunts. So I went into the palaestra of Taureas, which is over against the temple adjoining the porch of the King Archon, and there I found a number of persons, most of whom I knew, but not all. My visit was unexpected, and no sooner did they see me entering than they saluted me from afar on all sides; and Chaerephon, who is a kind of madman, started up and ran to me, seizing my hand, and saying, How did you escape, Socrates?—(I should explain that an engagement had taken place at Potidaea not long before we came away, of which the news had only just reached Athens.)

You see, I replied, that here I am.

There was a report, he said, that the engagement was very severe, and that many of our acquaintance had fallen.

That, I replied, was not far from the truth.

I suppose, he said, that you were present.

I was.

Then sit down, and tell us the whole story, which as yet we have only heard imperfectly.

I took the place which he assigned to me, by the side of Critias the son of Callaeschrus, and when I had saluted him and the rest of the company, I told them the news from the army, and answered their several enquiries.

Then, when there had been enough of this, I, in my turn, began to make enquiries about matters at home—about the present state of philosophy, and about the youth. I asked whether any of them were remarkable for wisdom or beauty, or both. Critias, glancing at the door, invited my attention to some youths who were coming in, and talking noisily to one another, followed by a crowd. Of the beauties, Socrates, he said, I fancy that you will soon be able to form a judgment. For those who are just entering are the advanced guard of the great beauty, as he is thought to be, of the day, and he is likely to be not far off himself.

Who is he, I said; and who is his father?

Charmides, he replied, is his name; he is my cousin, and the son of my uncle Glaucon: I rather think that you know him too, although he was not grown up at the time of your departure.

Certainly, I know him, I said, for he was remarkable even then when he was still a child, and I should imagine that by this time he must be almost a young man.

You will see, he said, in a moment what progress he has made and what he is like. He had scarcely said the word, when Charmides entered.

Now you know, my friend, that I cannot measure anything, and of the beautiful, I am simply such a measure as a white line is of chalk; for almost all young persons appear to be beautiful in my eyes. But at that moment, when I saw him coming in, I confess that I was quite astonished at his beauty and stature; all the world seemed to be enamoured of him; amazement and confusion reigned when he entered; and a troop of lovers followed him. That grown-up men like ourselves should have been affected in this way was not surprising, but I observed that there was the same feeling among the boys; all of them, down to the very least child, turned and looked at him, as if he had been a statue.

Chaerephon called me and said: What do you think of him, Socrates? Has he not a beautiful face?

Most beautiful, I said.

But you would think nothing of his face, he replied, if you could see his naked form: he is absolutely perfect.

And to this they all agreed.

By Heracles, I said, there never was such a paragon, if he has only one other slight addition.

What is that? said Critias.

If he has a noble soul; and being of your house, Critias, he may be expected to have this.

He is as fair and good within, as he is without, replied Critias.

Then, before we see his body, should we not ask him to show us his soul, naked and undisguised? he is just of an age at which he will like to talk.

That he will, said Critias, and I can tell you that he is a philosopher already, and also a considerable poet, not in his own opinion only, but in that of others.

That, my dear Critias, I replied, is a distinction which has long been in your family, and is inherited by you from Solon. But why do you not call him, and show him to us? for even if he were younger than he is, there could be no impropriety in his talking to us in the presence of you, who are his guardian and cousin.

Very well, he said; then I will call him; and turning to the attendant, he said, Call Charmides, and tell him that I want him to come and see a physician about the illness of which he spoke to me the day before yesterday. Then again addressing me, he added: He has been complaining lately of having a headache when he rises in the morning: now why should you not make him believe that you know a cure for the headache?

Why not, I said; but will he come?

He will be sure to come, he replied.

He came as he was bidden, and sat down between Critias and me. Great amusement was occasioned by every one pushing with might and main at his neighbour in order to make a place for him next to themselves, until at the two ends of the row one had to get up and the other was rolled over sideways. Now I, my friend, was beginning to feel awkward; my former bold belief in my powers of conversing with him had vanished. And when Critias told him that I was the person who had the cure, he looked at me in such an indescribable manner, and was just going to ask a question. And at that moment all the people in the palaestra crowded about us, and, O rare! I caught a sight of the inwards of his garment, and took the flame. Then I could no longer contain myself. I thought how well Cydias understood the nature of love, when, in speaking of a fair youth, he warns some one 'not to bring the fawn in the sight of the lion to be devoured by him,' for I felt that I had been overcome by a sort of wild-beast appetite. But I controlled myself, and when he asked me if I knew the cure of the headache, I answered, but with an effort, that I did know.

And what is it? he said.

I replied that it was a kind of leaf, which required to be accompanied by a charm, and if a person would repeat the charm at the same time that he used the cure, he would be made whole; but that without the charm the leaf would be of no avail.

Then I will write out the charm from your dictation, he said.

With my consent? I said, or without my consent?

With your consent, Socrates, he said, laughing.

Very good, I said; and are you quite sure that you know my name?

I ought to know you, he replied, for there is a great deal said about you among my companions; and I remember when I was a child seeing you in company with my cousin Critias.

I am glad to find that you remember me, I said; for I shall now be more at home with you and shall be better able to explain the nature of the charm, about which I felt a difficulty before. For the charm will do more, Charmides, than only cure the headache. I dare say that you have heard eminent physicians say to a patient who comes to them with bad eyes, that they cannot cure his eyes by themselves, but that if his eyes are to be cured, his head must be treated; and then again they say that to think of curing the head alone, and not the rest of the body also, is the height of folly. And arguing in this way they apply their methods to the whole body, and try to treat and heal the whole and the part together. Did you ever observe that this is what they say?

Yes, he said.

And they are right, and you would agree with them?

Yes, he said, certainly I should.

His approving answers reassured me, and I began by degrees to regain confidence, and the vital heat returned. Such, Charmides, I said, is the nature of the charm, which I learned when serving with the army from one of the physicians of the Thracian king Zamolxis, who are said to be so skilful that they can even give immortality. This Thracian told me that in these notions of theirs, which I was just now mentioning, the Greek physicians are quite right as far as they go; but Zamolxis, he added, our king, who is also a god, says further, 'that as you ought not to attempt to cure the eyes without the head, or the head without the body, so neither ought you to attempt to cure the body without the soul; and this,' he said, 'is the reason why the cure of many diseases is unknown to the physicians of Hellas, because they are ignorant of the whole, which ought to be studied also; for the part can never be well unless the whole is well.' For all good and evil, whether in the body or in human nature, originates, as he declared, in the soul, and overflows from thence, as if from the head into the eyes. And therefore if the head and body are to be well, you must begin by curing the soul; that is the first thing. And the cure, my dear youth, has to be effected by the use of certain charms, and these charms are fair words; and by them temperance is implanted in the soul, and where temperance is, there health is speedily imparted, not only to the head, but to the whole body. And he who taught me the cure and the charm at the same time added a special direction: 'Let no one,' he said, 'persuade you to cure the head, until he has first given you his soul to be cured by the charm. For this,' he said, 'is the great error of our day in the treatment of the human body, that physicians separate the soul from the body.' And he added with emphasis, at the same time making me swear to his words, 'Let no one, however rich, or noble, or fair, persuade you to give him the cure, without the charm.' Now I have sworn, and I must keep my oath, and therefore if you will allow me to apply the Thracian charm first to your soul, as the stranger directed, I will afterwards proceed to apply the cure to your head. But if not, I do not know what I am to do with you, my dear Charmides.

Critias, when he heard this, said: The headache will be an unexpected gain to my young relation, if the pain in his head compels him to improve his mind: and I can tell you, Socrates, that Charmides is not only pre-eminent in beauty among his equals, but also in that quality which is given by the charm; and this, as you say, is temperance?

Yes, I said.

Then let me tell you that he is the most temperate of human beings, and for his age inferior to none in any quality.

Yes, I said, Charmides; and indeed I think that you ought to excel others in all good qualities; for if I am not mistaken there is no one present who could easily point out two Athenian houses, whose union would be likely to produce a better or nobler scion than the two from which you are sprung. There is your father's house, which is descended from Critias the son of Dropidas, whose family has been commemorated in the panegyrical verses of Anacreon, Solon, and many other poets, as famous for beauty and virtue and all other high fortune: and your mother's house is equally distinguished; for your maternal uncle, Pyrilampes, is reputed never to have found his equal, in Persia at the court of the great king, or on the continent of Asia, in all the places to which he went as ambassador, for stature and beauty; that whole family is not a whit inferior to the other. Having such ancestors you ought to be first in all things, and, sweet son of Glaucon, your outward form is no dishonour to any of them. If to beauty you add temperance, and if in other respects you are what Critias declares you to be, then, dear Charmides, blessed art thou, in being the son of thy mother. And here lies the point; for if, as he declares, you have this gift of temperance already, and are temperate enough, in that case you have no need of any charms, whether of Zamolxis or of Abaris the Hyperborean, and I may as well let you have the cure of the head at once; but if you have not yet acquired this quality, I must use the charm before I give you the medicine. Please, therefore, to inform me whether you admit the truth of what Critias has been saying;—have you or have you not this quality of temperance?

Charmides blushed, and the blush heightened his beauty, for modesty is becoming in youth; he then said very ingenuously, that he really could not at once answer, either yes, or no, to the question which I had asked: For, said he, if I affirm that I am not temperate, that would be a strange thing for me to say of myself, and also I should give the lie to Critias, and many others who think as he tells you, that I am temperate: but, on the other hand, if I say that I am, I shall have to praise myself, which would be ill manners; and therefore I do not know how to answer you.

I said to him: That is a natural reply, Charmides, and I think that you and I ought together to enquire whether you have this quality about which I am asking or not; and then you will not be compelled to say what you do not like; neither shall I be a rash practitioner of medicine: therefore, if you please, I will share the enquiry with you, but I will not press you if you would rather not.

There is nothing which I should like better, he said; and as far as I am concerned you may proceed in the way which you think best.

I think, I said, that I had better begin by asking you a question; for if temperance abides in you, you must have an opinion about her; she must give some intimation of her nature and qualities, which may enable you to form a notion of her. Is not that true?

Yes, he said, that I think is true.

You know your native language, I said, and therefore you must be able to tell what you feel about this.

Certainly, he said.

In order, then, that I may form a conjecture whether you have temperance abiding in you or not, tell me, I said, what, in your opinion, is Temperance?

At first he hesitated, and was very unwilling to answer: then he said that he thought temperance was doing things orderly and quietly, such things for example as walking in the streets, and talking, or anything else of that nature. In a word, he said, I should answer that, in my opinion, temperance is quietness.

Are you right, Charmides? I said. No doubt some would affirm that the quiet are the temperate; but let us see whether these words have any meaning; and first tell me whether you would not acknowledge temperance to be of the class of the noble and good?

Yes.

But which is best when you are at the writing-master's, to write the same letters quickly or quietly?

Quickly.

And to read quickly or slowly?

Quickly again.

And in playing the lyre, or wrestling, quickness or sharpness are far better than quietness and slowness?

Yes.

And the same holds in boxing and in the pancratium?

Certainly.

And in leaping and running and in bodily exercises generally, quickness and agility are good; slowness, and inactivity, and quietness, are bad?

That is evident.

Then, I said, in all bodily actions, not quietness, but the greatest agility and quickness, is noblest and best?

Yes, certainly.

And is temperance a good?

Yes.

Then, in reference to the body, not quietness, but quickness will be the higher degree of temperance, if temperance is a good?

True, he said.

And which, I said, is better—facility in learning, or difficulty in learning?

Facility.

Yes, I said; and facility in learning is learning quickly, and difficulty in learning is learning quietly and slowly?

True.

And is it not better to teach another quickly and energetically, rather than quietly and slowly?

Yes.

And which is better, to call to mind, and to remember, quickly and readily, or quietly and slowly?

The former.

And is not shrewdness a quickness or cleverness of the soul, and not a quietness?

True.

And is it not best to understand what is said, whether at the writing-master's or the music-master's, or anywhere else, not as quietly as possible, but as quickly as possible?

Yes.

And in the searchings or deliberations of the soul, not the quietest, as I imagine, and he who with difficulty deliberates and discovers, is thought worthy of praise, but he who does so most easily and quickly?

Quite true, he said.

And in all that concerns either body or soul, swiftness and activity are clearly better than slowness and quietness?

Clearly they are.

Then temperance is not quietness, nor is the temperate life quiet,—certainly not upon this view; for the life which is temperate is supposed to be the good. And of two things, one is true,—either never, or very seldom, do the quiet actions in life appear to be better than the quick and energetic ones; or supposing that of the nobler actions, there are as many quiet, as quick and vehement: still, even if we grant this, temperance will not be acting quietly any more than acting quickly and energetically, either in walking or talking or in anything else; nor will the quiet life be more temperate than the unquiet, seeing that temperance is admitted by us to be a good and noble thing, and the quick have been shown to be as good as the quiet.

I think, he said, Socrates, that you are right.

Then once more, Charmides, I said, fix your attention, and look within; consider the effect which temperance has upon yourself, and the nature of that which has the effect. Think over all this, and, like a brave youth, tell me—What is temperance?

After a moment's pause, in which he made a real manly effort to think, he said: My opinion is, Socrates, that temperance makes a man ashamed or modest, and that temperance is the same as modesty.

Very good, I said; and did you not admit, just now, that temperance is noble?

Yes, certainly, he said.

And the temperate are also good?

Yes.

And can that be good which does not make men good?

Certainly not.

And you would infer that temperance is not only noble, but also good?

That is my opinion.

Well, I said; but surely you would agree with Homer when he says,

'Modesty is not good for a needy man'?

Yes, he said; I agree.

Then I suppose that modesty is and is not good?

Clearly.

But temperance, whose presence makes men only good, and not bad, is always good?

That appears to me to be as you say.

And the inference is that temperance cannot be modesty—if temperance is a good, and if modesty is as much an evil as a good?

All that, Socrates, appears to me to be true; but I should like to know what you think about another definition of temperance, which I just now remember to have heard from some one, who said, 'That temperance is doing our own business.' Was he right who affirmed that?

You monster! I said; this is what Critias, or some philosopher has told you.

Some one else, then, said Critias; for certainly I have not.

But what matter, said Charmides, from whom I heard this?

No matter at all, I replied; for the point is not who said the words, but whether they are true or not.

There you are in the right, Socrates, he replied.

To be sure, I said; yet I doubt whether we shall ever be able to discover their truth or falsehood; for they are a kind of riddle.

What makes you think so? he said.

Because, I said, he who uttered them seems to me to have meant one thing, and said another. Is the scribe, for example, to be regarded as doing nothing when he reads or writes?

I should rather think that he was doing something.

And does the scribe write or read, or teach you boys to write or read, your own names only, or did you write your enemies' names as well as your own and your friends'?

As much one as the other.

And was there anything meddling or intemperate in this?

Certainly not.

And yet if reading and writing are the same as doing, you were doing what was not your own business?

But they are the same as doing.

And the healing art, my friend, and building, and weaving, and doing anything whatever which is done by art,—these all clearly come under the head of doing?

Certainly.

And do you think that a state would be well ordered by a law which compelled every man to weave and wash his own coat, and make his own shoes, and his own flask and strigil, and other implements, on this principle of every one doing and performing his own, and abstaining from what is not his own?

I think not, he said.

But, I said, a temperate state will be a well-ordered state.

Of course, he replied.

Then temperance, I said, will not be doing one's own business; not at least in this way, or doing things of this sort?

Clearly not.

Then, as I was just now saying, he who declared that temperance is a man doing his own business had another and a hidden meaning; for I do not think that he could have been such a fool as to mean this. Was he a fool who told you, Charmides?

Nay, he replied, I certainly thought him a very wise man.

Then I am quite certain that he put forth his definition as a riddle, thinking that no one would know the meaning of the words 'doing his own business.'

I dare say, he replied.

And what is the meaning of a man doing his own business? Can you tell me?

Indeed, I cannot; and I should not wonder if the man himself who used this phrase did not understand what he was saying. Whereupon he laughed slyly, and looked at Critias.

Critias had long been showing uneasiness, for he felt that he had a reputation to maintain with Charmides and the rest of the company. He had, however, hitherto managed to restrain himself; but now he could no longer forbear, and I am convinced of the truth of the suspicion which I entertained at the time, that Charmides had heard this answer about temperance from Critias. And Charmides, who did not want to answer himself, but to make Critias answer, tried to stir him up. He went on pointing out that he had been refuted, at which Critias grew angry, and appeared, as I thought, inclined to quarrel with him; just as a poet might quarrel with an actor who spoiled his poems in repeating them; so he looked hard at him and said—

Do you imagine, Charmides, that the author of this definition of temperance did not understand the meaning of his own words, because you do not understand them?

Why, at his age, I said, most excellent Critias, he can hardly be expected to understand; but you, who are older, and have studied, may well be assumed to know the meaning of them; and therefore, if you agree with him, and accept his definition of temperance, I would much rather argue with you than with him about the truth or falsehood of the definition.

I entirely agree, said Critias, and accept the definition.

Very good, I said; and now let me repeat my question—Do you admit, as I was just now saying, that all craftsmen make or do something?

I do.

And do they make or do their own business only, or that of others also?

They make or do that of others also.

And are they temperate, seeing that they make not for themselves or their own business only?

Why not? he said.

No objection on my part, I said, but there may be a difficulty on his who proposes as a definition of temperance, 'doing one's own business,' and then says that there is no reason why those who do the business of others should not be temperate.

Nay (The English reader has to observe that the word 'make' (Greek), in Greek, has also the sense of 'do' (Greek).), said he; did I ever acknowledge that those who do the business of others are temperate? I said, those who make, not those who do.

What! I asked; do you mean to say that doing and making are not the same?

No more, he replied, than making or working are the same; thus much I have learned from Hesiod, who says that 'work is no disgrace.' Now do you imagine that if he had meant by working and doing such things as you were describing, he would have said that there was no disgrace in them—for example, in the manufacture of shoes, or in selling pickles, or sitting for hire in a house of ill-fame? That, Socrates, is not to be supposed: but I conceive him to have distinguished making from doing and work; and, while admitting that the making anything might sometimes become a disgrace, when the employment was not honourable, to have thought that work was never any disgrace at all. For things nobly and usefully made he called works; and such makings he called workings, and doings; and he must be supposed to have called such things only man's proper business, and what is hurtful, not his business: and in that sense Hesiod, and any other wise man, may be reasonably supposed to call him wise who does his own work.

O Critias, I said, no sooner had you opened your mouth, than I pretty well knew that you would call that which is proper to a man, and that which is his own, good; and that the makings (Greek) of the good you would call doings (Greek), for I am no stranger to the endless distinctions which Prodicus draws about names. Now I have no objection to your giving names any signification which you please, if you will only tell me what you mean by them. Please then to begin again, and be a little plainer. Do you mean that this doing or making, or whatever is the word which you would use, of good actions, is temperance?

I do, he said.

Then not he who does evil, but he who does good, is temperate?

Yes, he said; and you, friend, would agree.

No matter whether I should or not; just now, not what I think, but what you are saying, is the point at issue.

Well, he answered; I mean to say, that he who does evil, and not good, is not temperate; and that he is temperate who does good, and not evil: for temperance I define in plain words to be the doing of good actions.

And you may be very likely right in what you are saying; but I am curious to know whether you imagine that temperate men are ignorant of their own temperance?

I do not think so, he said.

And yet were you not saying, just now, that craftsmen might be temperate in doing another's work, as well as in doing their own?

I was, he replied; but what is your drift?

I have no particular drift, but I wish that you would tell me whether a physician who cures a patient may do good to himself and good to another also?

I think that he may.

And he who does so does his duty?

Yes.

And does not he who does his duty act temperately or wisely?

Yes, he acts wisely.

But must the physician necessarily know when his treatment is likely to prove beneficial, and when not? or must the craftsman necessarily know when he is likely to be benefited, and when not to be benefited, by the work which he is doing?

I suppose not.

Then, I said, he may sometimes do good or harm, and not know what he is himself doing, and yet, in doing good, as you say, he has done temperately or wisely. Was not that your statement?

Yes.

Then, as would seem, in doing good, he may act wisely or temperately, and be wise or temperate, but not know his own wisdom or temperance?

But that, Socrates, he said, is impossible; and therefore if this is, as you imply, the necessary consequence of any of my previous admissions, I will withdraw them, rather than admit that a man can be temperate or wise who does not know himself; and I am not ashamed to confess that I was in error. For self-knowledge would certainly be maintained by me to be the very essence of knowledge, and in this I agree with him who dedicated the inscription, 'Know thyself!' at Delphi. That word, if I am not mistaken, is put there as a sort of salutation which the god addresses to those who enter the temple; as much as to say that the ordinary salutation of 'Hail!' is not right, and that the exhortation 'Be temperate!' would be a far better way of saluting one another. The notion of him who dedicated the inscription was, as I believe, that the god speaks to those who enter his temple, not as men speak; but, when a worshipper enters, the first word which he hears is 'Be temperate!' This, however, like a prophet he expresses in a sort of riddle, for 'Know thyself!' and 'Be temperate!' are the same, as I maintain, and as the letters imply (Greek), and yet they may be easily misunderstood; and succeeding sages who added 'Never too much,' or, 'Give a pledge, and evil is nigh at hand,' would appear to have so misunderstood them; for they imagined that 'Know thyself!' was a piece of advice which the god gave, and not his salutation of the worshippers at their first coming in; and they dedicated their own inscription under the idea that they too would give equally useful pieces of advice. Shall I tell you, Socrates, why I say all this? My object is to leave the previous discussion (in which I know not whether you or I are more right, but, at any rate, no clear result was attained), and to raise a new one in which I will attempt to prove, if you deny, that temperance is self-knowledge.

Yes, I said, Critias; but you come to me as though I professed to know about the questions which I ask, and as though I could, if I only would, agree with you. Whereas the fact is that I enquire with you into the truth of that which is advanced from time to time, just because I do not know; and when I have enquired, I will say whether I agree with you or not. Please then to allow me time to reflect.

Reflect, he said.

I am reflecting, I replied, and discover that temperance, or wisdom, if implying a knowledge of anything, must be a science, and a science of something.

Yes, he said; the science of itself.

Is not medicine, I said, the science of health?

True.

And suppose, I said, that I were asked by you what is the use or effect of medicine, which is this science of health, I should answer that medicine is of very great use in producing health, which, as you will admit, is an excellent effect.

Granted.

And if you were to ask me, what is the result or effect of architecture, which is the science of building, I should say houses, and so of other arts, which all have their different results. Now I want you, Critias, to answer a similar question about temperance, or wisdom, which, according to you, is the science of itself. Admitting this view, I ask of you, what good work, worthy of the name wise, does temperance or wisdom, which is the science of itself, effect? Answer me.

That is not the true way of pursuing the enquiry, Socrates, he said; for wisdom is not like the other sciences, any more than they are like one another: but you proceed as if they were alike. For tell me, he said, what result is there of computation or geometry, in the same sense as a house is the result of building, or a garment of weaving, or any other work of any other art? Can you show me any such result of them? You cannot.

That is true, I said; but still each of these sciences has a subject which is different from the science. I can show you that the art of computation has to do with odd and even numbers in their numerical relations to themselves and to each other. Is not that true?

Yes, he said.

And the odd and even numbers are not the same with the art of computation?

They are not.

The art of weighing, again, has to do with lighter and heavier; but the art of weighing is one thing, and the heavy and the light another. Do you admit that?

Yes.

Now, I want to know, what is that which is not wisdom, and of which wisdom is the science?

You are just falling into the old error, Socrates, he said. You come asking in what wisdom or temperance differs from the other sciences, and then you try to discover some respect in which they are alike; but they are not, for all the other sciences are of something else, and not of themselves; wisdom alone is a science of other sciences, and of itself. And of this, as I believe, you are very well aware: and that you are only doing what you denied that you were doing just now, trying to refute me, instead of pursuing the argument.

And what if I am? How can you think that I have any other motive in refuting you but what I should have in examining into myself? which motive would be just a fear of my unconsciously fancying that I knew something of which I was ignorant. And at this moment I pursue the argument chiefly for my own sake, and perhaps in some degree also for the sake of my other friends. For is not the discovery of things as they truly are, a good common to all mankind?

Yes, certainly, Socrates, he said.

Then, I said, be cheerful, sweet sir, and give your opinion in answer to the question which I asked, never minding whether Critias or Socrates is the person refuted; attend only to the argument, and see what will come of the refutation.

I think that you are right, he replied; and I will do as you say.

Tell me, then, I said, what you mean to affirm about wisdom.

I mean to say that wisdom is the only science which is the science of itself as well as of the other sciences.

But the science of science, I said, will also be the science of the absence of science.

Very true, he said.

Then the wise or temperate man, and he only, will know himself, and be able to examine what he knows or does not know, and to see what others know and think that they know and do really know; and what they do not know, and fancy that they know, when they do not. No other person will be able to do this. And this is wisdom and temperance and self-knowledge—for a man to know what he knows, and what he does not know. That is your meaning?

Yes, he said.

Now then, I said, making an offering of the third or last argument to Zeus the Saviour, let us begin again, and ask, in the first place, whether it is or is not possible for a person to know that he knows and does not know what he knows and does not know; and in the second place, whether, if perfectly possible, such knowledge is of any use.

That is what we have to consider, he said.

And here, Critias, I said, I hope that you will find a way out of a difficulty into which I have got myself. Shall I tell you the nature of the difficulty?

By all means, he replied.

Does not what you have been saying, if true, amount to this: that there must be a single science which is wholly a science of itself and of other sciences, and that the same is also the science of the absence of science?

Yes.

But consider how monstrous this proposition is, my friend: in any parallel case, the impossibility will be transparent to you.

How is that? and in what cases do you mean?

In such cases as this: Suppose that there is a kind of vision which is not like ordinary vision, but a vision of itself and of other sorts of vision, and of the defect of them, which in seeing sees no colour, but only itself and other sorts of vision: Do you think that there is such a kind of vision?

Certainly not.

Or is there a kind of hearing which hears no sound at all, but only itself and other sorts of hearing, or the defects of them?

There is not.

Or take all the senses: can you imagine that there is any sense of itself and of other senses, but which is incapable of perceiving the objects of the senses?

I think not.

Could there be any desire which is not the desire of any pleasure, but of itself, and of all other desires?

Certainly not.

Or can you imagine a wish which wishes for no good, but only for itself and all other wishes?

I should answer, No.

Or would you say that there is a love which is not the love of beauty, but of itself and of other loves?

I should not.

Or did you ever know of a fear which fears itself or other fears, but has no object of fear?

I never did, he said.

Or of an opinion which is an opinion of itself and of other opinions, and which has no opinion on the subjects of opinion in general?

Certainly not.

But surely we are assuming a science of this kind, which, having no subject-matter, is a science of itself and of the other sciences?

Yes, that is what is affirmed.

But how strange is this, if it be indeed true: we must not however as yet absolutely deny the possibility of such a science; let us rather consider the matter.

You are quite right.

Well then, this science of which we are speaking is a science of something, and is of a nature to be a science of something?

Yes.

Just as that which is greater is of a nature to be greater than something else? (Socrates is intending to show that science differs from the object of science, as any other relative differs from the object of relation. But where there is comparison—greater, less, heavier, lighter, and the like—a relation to self as well as to other things involves an absolute contradiction; and in other cases, as in the case of the senses, is hardly conceivable. The use of the genitive after the comparative in Greek, (Greek), creates an unavoidable obscurity in the translation.)

Yes.

Which is less, if the other is conceived to be greater?

To be sure.

And if we could find something which is at once greater than itself, and greater than other great things, but not greater than those things in comparison of which the others are greater, then that thing would have the property of being greater and also less than itself?

That, Socrates, he said, is the inevitable inference.

Or if there be a double which is double of itself and of other doubles, these will be halves; for the double is relative to the half?

That is true.

And that which is greater than itself will also be less, and that which is heavier will also be lighter, and that which is older will also be younger: and the same of other things; that which has a nature relative to self will retain also the nature of its object: I mean to say, for example, that hearing is, as we say, of sound or voice. Is that true?

Yes.

Then if hearing hears itself, it must hear a voice; for there is no other way of hearing.

Certainly.

And sight also, my excellent friend, if it sees itself must see a colour, for sight cannot see that which has no colour.

No.

Do you remark, Critias, that in several of the examples which have been recited the notion of a relation to self is altogether inadmissible, and in other cases hardly credible—inadmissible, for example, in the case of magnitudes, numbers, and the like?

Very true.

But in the case of hearing and sight, or in the power of self-motion, and the power of heat to burn, this relation to self will be regarded as incredible by some, but perhaps not by others. And some great man, my friend, is wanted, who will satisfactorily determine for us, whether there is nothing which has an inherent property of relation to self, or some things only and not others; and whether in this class of self-related things, if there be such a class, that science which is called wisdom or temperance is included. I altogether distrust my own power of determining these matters: I am not certain whether there is such a science of science at all; and even if there be, I should not acknowledge this to be wisdom or temperance, until I can also see whether such a science would or would not do us any good; for I have an impression that temperance is a benefit and a good. And therefore, O son of Callaeschrus, as you maintain that temperance or wisdom is a science of science, and also of the absence of science, I will request you to show in the first place, as I was saying before, the possibility, and in the second place, the advantage, of such a science; and then perhaps you may satisfy me that you are right in your view of temperance.

Critias heard me say this, and saw that I was in a difficulty; and as one person when another yawns in his presence catches the infection of yawning from him, so did he seem to be driven into a difficulty by my difficulty. But as he had a reputation to maintain, he was ashamed to admit before the company that he could not answer my challenge or determine the question at issue; and he made an unintelligible attempt to hide his perplexity. In order that the argument might proceed, I said to him, Well then Critias, if you like, let us assume that there is this science of science; whether the assumption is right or wrong may hereafter be investigated. Admitting the existence of it, will you tell me how such a science enables us to distinguish what we know or do not know, which, as we were saying, is self-knowledge or wisdom: so we were saying?

Yes, Socrates, he said; and that I think is certainly true: for he who has this science or knowledge which knows itself will become like the knowledge which he has, in the same way that he who has swiftness will be swift, and he who has beauty will be beautiful, and he who has knowledge will know. In the same way he who has that knowledge which is self-knowing, will know himself.

I do not doubt, I said, that a man will know himself, when he possesses that which has self-knowledge: but what necessity is there that, having this, he should know what he knows and what he does not know?

Because, Socrates, they are the same.

Very likely, I said; but I remain as stupid as ever; for still I fail to comprehend how this knowing what you know and do not know is the same as the knowledge of self.

What do you mean? he said.

This is what I mean, I replied: I will admit that there is a science of science;—can this do more than determine that of two things one is and the other is not science or knowledge?

No, just that.

But is knowledge or want of knowledge of health the same as knowledge or want of knowledge of justice?

Certainly not.

The one is medicine, and the other is politics; whereas that of which we are speaking is knowledge pure and simple.

Very true.

And if a man knows only, and has only knowledge of knowledge, and has no further knowledge of health and justice, the probability is that he will only know that he knows something, and has a certain knowledge, whether concerning himself or other men.

True.

Then how will this knowledge or science teach him to know what he knows? Say that he knows health;—not wisdom or temperance, but the art of medicine has taught it to him;—and he has learned harmony from the art of music, and building from the art of building,—neither, from wisdom or temperance: and the same of other things.

That is evident.

How will wisdom, regarded only as a knowledge of knowledge or science of science, ever teach him that he knows health, or that he knows building?

It is impossible.

Then he who is ignorant of these things will only know that he knows, but not what he knows?

True.

Then wisdom or being wise appears to be not the knowledge of the things which we do or do not know, but only the knowledge that we know or do not know?

That is the inference.

Then he who has this knowledge will not be able to examine whether a pretender knows or does not know that which he says that he knows: he will only know that he has a knowledge of some kind; but wisdom will not show him of what the knowledge is?

Plainly not.

Neither will he be able to distinguish the pretender in medicine from the true physician, nor between any other true and false professor of knowledge. Let us consider the matter in this way: If the wise man or any other man wants to distinguish the true physician from the false, how will he proceed? He will not talk to him about medicine; and that, as we were saying, is the only thing which the physician understands.

True.

And, on the other hand, the physician knows nothing of science, for this has been assumed to be the province of wisdom.

True.

And further, since medicine is science, we must infer that he does not know anything of medicine.

Exactly.

Then the wise man may indeed know that the physician has some kind of science or knowledge; but when he wants to discover the nature of this he will ask, What is the subject-matter? For the several sciences are distinguished not by the mere fact that they are sciences, but by the nature of their subjects. Is not that true?

Quite true.

And medicine is distinguished from other sciences as having the subject-matter of health and disease?

Yes.

And he who would enquire into the nature of medicine must pursue the enquiry into health and disease, and not into what is extraneous?

True.

And he who judges rightly will judge of the physician as a physician in what relates to these?

He will.

He will consider whether what he says is true, and whether what he does is right, in relation to health and disease?

He will.

But can any one attain the knowledge of either unless he have a knowledge of medicine?

He cannot.

No one at all, it would seem, except the physician can have this knowledge; and therefore not the wise man; he would have to be a physician as well as a wise man.

Very true.

Then, assuredly, wisdom or temperance, if only a science of science, and of the absence of science or knowledge, will not be able to distinguish the physician who knows from one who does not know but pretends or thinks that he knows, or any other professor of anything at all; like any other artist, he will only know his fellow in art or wisdom, and no one else.

That is evident, he said.

But then what profit, Critias, I said, is there any longer in wisdom or temperance which yet remains, if this is wisdom? If, indeed, as we were supposing at first, the wise man had been able to distinguish what he knew and did not know, and that he knew the one and did not know the other, and to recognize a similar faculty of discernment in others, there would certainly have been a great advantage in being wise; for then we should never have made a mistake, but have passed through life the unerring guides of ourselves and of those who are under us; and we should not have attempted to do what we did not know, but we should have found out those who knew, and have handed the business over to them and trusted in them; nor should we have allowed those who were under us to do anything which they were not likely to do well; and they would be likely to do well just that of which they had knowledge; and the house or state which was ordered or administered under the guidance of wisdom, and everything else of which wisdom was the lord, would have been well ordered; for truth guiding, and error having been eliminated, in all their doings, men would have done well, and would have been happy. Was not this, Critias, what we spoke of as the great advantage of wisdom—to know what is known and what is unknown to us?

Very true, he said.

And now you perceive, I said, that no such science is to be found anywhere.

I perceive, he said.

May we assume then, I said, that wisdom, viewed in this new light merely as a knowledge of knowledge and ignorance, has this advantage:—that he who possesses such knowledge will more easily learn anything which he learns; and that everything will be clearer to him, because, in addition to the knowledge of individuals, he sees the science, and this also will better enable him to test the knowledge which others have of what he knows himself; whereas the enquirer who is without this knowledge may be supposed to have a feebler and weaker insight? Are not these, my friend, the real advantages which are to be gained from wisdom? And are not we looking and seeking after something more than is to be found in her?

That is very likely, he said.

That is very likely, I said; and very likely, too, we have been enquiring to no purpose; as I am led to infer, because I observe that if this is wisdom, some strange consequences would follow. Let us, if you please, assume the possibility of this science of sciences, and further admit and allow, as was originally suggested, that wisdom is the knowledge of what we know and do not know. Assuming all this, still, upon further consideration, I am doubtful, Critias, whether wisdom, such as this, would do us much good. For we were wrong, I think, in supposing, as we were saying just now, that such wisdom ordering the government of house or state would be a great benefit.

How so? he said.

Why, I said, we were far too ready to admit the great benefits which mankind would obtain from their severally doing the things which they knew, and committing the things of which they are ignorant to those who were better acquainted with them.

Were we not right in making that admission?

I think not.

How very strange, Socrates!

By the dog of Egypt, I said, there I agree with you; and I was thinking as much just now when I said that strange consequences would follow, and that I was afraid we were on the wrong track; for however ready we may be to admit that this is wisdom, I certainly cannot make out what good this sort of thing does to us.

What do you mean? he said; I wish that you could make me understand what you mean.

I dare say that what I am saying is nonsense, I replied; and yet if a man has any feeling of what is due to himself, he cannot let the thought which comes into his mind pass away unheeded and unexamined.

I like that, he said.

Hear, then, I said, my own dream; whether coming through the horn or the ivory gate, I cannot tell. The dream is this: Let us suppose that wisdom is such as we are now defining, and that she has absolute sway over us; then each action will be done according to the arts or sciences, and no one professing to be a pilot when he is not, or any physician or general, or any one else pretending to know matters of which he is ignorant, will deceive or elude us; our health will be improved; our safety at sea, and also in battle, will be assured; our coats and shoes, and all other instruments and implements will be skilfully made, because the workmen will be good and true. Aye, and if you please, you may suppose that prophecy, which is the knowledge of the future, will be under the control of wisdom, and that she will deter deceivers and set up the true prophets in their place as the revealers of the future. Now I quite agree that mankind, thus provided, would live and act according to knowledge, for wisdom would watch and prevent ignorance from intruding on us. But whether by acting according to knowledge we shall act well and be happy, my dear Critias,—this is a point which we have not yet been able to determine.

Yet I think, he replied, that if you discard knowledge, you will hardly find the crown of happiness in anything else.

But of what is this knowledge? I said. Just answer me that small question. Do you mean a knowledge of shoemaking?

God forbid.

Or of working in brass?

Certainly not.

Or in wool, or wood, or anything of that sort?

No, I do not.

Then, I said, we are giving up the doctrine that he who lives according to knowledge is happy, for these live according to knowledge, and yet they are not allowed by you to be happy; but I think that you mean to confine happiness to particular individuals who live according to knowledge, such for example as the prophet, who, as I was saying, knows the future. Is it of him you are speaking or of some one else?

Yes, I mean him, but there are others as well.

Yes, I said, some one who knows the past and present as well as the future, and is ignorant of nothing. Let us suppose that there is such a person, and if there is, you will allow that he is the most knowing of all living men.

Certainly he is.

Yet I should like to know one thing more: which of the different kinds of knowledge makes him happy? or do all equally make him happy?

Not all equally, he replied.

But which most tends to make him happy? the knowledge of what past, present, or future thing? May I infer this to be the knowledge of the game of draughts?

Nonsense about the game of draughts.

Or of computation?

No.

Or of health?

That is nearer the truth, he said.

And that knowledge which is nearest of all, I said, is the knowledge of what?

The knowledge with which he discerns good and evil.

Monster! I said; you have been carrying me round in a circle, and all this time hiding from me the fact that the life according to knowledge is not that which makes men act rightly and be happy, not even if knowledge include all the sciences, but one science only, that of good and evil. For, let me ask you, Critias, whether, if you take away this, medicine will not equally give health, and shoemaking equally produce shoes, and the art of the weaver clothes?—whether the art of the pilot will not equally save our lives at sea, and the art of the general in war?

Quite so.

And yet, my dear Critias, none of these things will be well or beneficially done, if the science of the good be wanting.

True.

But that science is not wisdom or temperance, but a science of human advantage; not a science of other sciences, or of ignorance, but of good and evil: and if this be of use, then wisdom or temperance will not be of use.

And why, he replied, will not wisdom be of use? For, however much we assume that wisdom is a science of sciences, and has a sway over other sciences, surely she will have this particular science of the good under her control, and in this way will benefit us.

And will wisdom give health? I said; is not this rather the effect of medicine? Or does wisdom do the work of any of the other arts,—do they not each of them do their own work? Have we not long ago asseverated that wisdom is only the knowledge of knowledge and of ignorance, and of nothing else?

That is obvious.

Then wisdom will not be the producer of health.

Certainly not.

The art of health is different.

Yes, different.

Nor does wisdom give advantage, my good friend; for that again we have just now been attributing to another art.

Very true.

How then can wisdom be advantageous, when giving no advantage?

That, Socrates, is certainly inconceivable.

You see then, Critias, that I was not far wrong in fearing that I could have no sound notion about wisdom; I was quite right in depreciating myself; for that which is admitted to be the best of all things would never have seemed to us useless, if I had been good for anything at an enquiry. But now I have been utterly defeated, and have failed to discover what that is to which the imposer of names gave this name of temperance or wisdom. And yet many more admissions were made by us than could be fairly granted; for we admitted that there was a science of science, although the argument said No, and protested against us; and we admitted further, that this science knew the works of the other sciences (although this too was denied by the argument), because we wanted to show that the wise man had knowledge of what he knew and did not know; also we nobly disregarded, and never even considered, the impossibility of a man knowing in a sort of way that which he does not know at all; for our assumption was, that he knows that which he does not know; than which nothing, as I think, can be more irrational. And yet, after finding us so easy and good-natured, the enquiry is still unable to discover the truth; but mocks us to a degree, and has gone out of its way to prove the inutility of that which we admitted only by a sort of supposition and fiction to be the true definition of temperance or wisdom: which result, as far as I am concerned, is not so much to be lamented, I said. But for your sake, Charmides, I am very sorry—that you, having such beauty and such wisdom and temperance of soul, should have no profit or good in life from your wisdom and temperance. And still more am I grieved about the charm which I learned with so much pain, and to so little profit, from the Thracian, for the sake of a thing which is nothing worth. I think indeed that there is a mistake, and that I must be a bad enquirer, for wisdom or temperance I believe to be really a great good; and happy are you, Charmides, if you certainly possess it. Wherefore examine yourself, and see whether you have this gift and can do without the charm; for if you can, I would rather advise you to regard me simply as a fool who is never able to reason out anything; and to rest assured that the more wise and temperate you are, the happier you will be.

Charmides said: I am sure that I do not know, Socrates, whether I have or have not this gift of wisdom and temperance; for how can I know whether I have a thing, of which even you and Critias are, as you say, unable to discover the nature?—(not that I believe you.) And further, I am sure, Socrates, that I do need the charm, and as far as I am concerned, I shall be willing to be charmed by you daily, until you say that I have had enough.

Very good, Charmides, said Critias; if you do this I shall have a proof of your temperance, that is, if you allow yourself to be charmed by Socrates, and never desert him at all.

You may depend on my following and not deserting him, said Charmides: if you who are my guardian command me, I should be very wrong not to obey you.

And I do command you, he said.

Then I will do as you say, and begin this very day.

You sirs, I said, what are you conspiring about?

We are not conspiring, said Charmides, we have conspired already.

And are you about to use violence, without even going through the forms of justice?

Yes, I shall use violence, he replied, since he orders me; and therefore you had better consider well.

But the time for consideration has passed, I said, when violence is employed; and you, when you are determined on anything, and in the mood of violence, are irresistible.

Do not you resist me then, he said.

I will not resist you, I replied.

Plato – A Short Biography

For someone whose influence has been so profound on Western thinking remarkably little is known of him.

There is still much discussion as to when and where he was born. It is almost certain that he was born into an influential and aristocratic family. As to where it seems to be Athens although others have claimed it might be Aegina, one of the Saroinc Islands in the Saronic Gulf, 27 kilometres from Athens.

With such a lack of detail on Plato's life scholars have tried to re-construct parts of the timeline using his writings, those of his contemporaries and histories of the time. Even so much is open to debate.

Traditional history estimates Plato's birth was around 428 B.C.E., but increasingly among more modern scholars, they conclude he was born between 424 and 423 B.C.E. Both of his parents came from the Greek aristocracy. Plato's father, Ariston, was descended from the kings of Athens and Messenia. His mother, Perictione, was claimed to be related to the 6th century B.C.E. Greek statesman Solon.

Due to the means and social status of his family Plato was most probably educated by some of Athens' finest teachers. The curriculum would have been rich and varied and include the doctrines of Cratylus and Pythagoras as well as Parmenides.

Plato's father, Ariston, died when he was still a boy. His mother re-married to her uncle, Pyrilampes, a politician and ambassador to Persia.

It is thought that Plato had several siblings; two brothers, a sister and a half-brother, though it is not confirmed where Plato falls in this line. From his dialogues though it is certain that he holds them in fond affection and introduces them in several.

Two major events shaped Plato's life whilst he was a young man. The first was a meeting with the great philosopher Socrates. Socrates's methods of debate impressed Plato and he soon became a devoted follower. From here would flow Plato's career as one of the finest minds civilization has produced.

Major event number two was the on-going rivalry between Athens and Sparta which erupted into the Peloponnesian War. This was in fact several 'stop-start' wars fought during the period 431–404 BCE. Plato served in the cause of Athens and its Allies between 409 and 404 B.C.E.

The comprehensive defeat of Athens by the Peloponnesian League led by Sparta ended the Athenian democracy. It was replaced by a Spartan imposed oligarchy. Ironically two of Plato's relatives, Charmides and Critias, were now prominent figures in the new government, known as the Thirty Tyrants whose brief 8 month rule severely reduced the rights of Athenian citizens as well as slaughtering somewhere in the region of 5% of their number.

After the oligarchy was overthrown and the former institutions of Athens began their slow rebuilding, Plato briefly considered a career in politics, but the execution of Socrates in 399 B.C.E., after being found guilty on the twin charges of moral corruption and impiety, discouraged Plato away from this idea and he turned to a life of study and philosophy.

Plato now traveled for a dozen years throughout the Mediterranean, studying mathematics with the Pythagoreans in Italy, as well as geometry, geology, astronomy and religion in Egypt. It was during this time that Plato began his writings, a remarkable number of which survive to this day.

The writings themselves are usually classified into three distinct periods although there is some uncertainty as to the exact order in which they were written.

The first, or early, period occurs during Plato's travels (399-387 B.C.E.). The Apology of Socrates appears to have been written shortly after Socrates's death. Other texts included in this period include Protagoras, Euthyphro, Hippias Major and Minor and Ion. It is in these dialogues, Plato attempts to convey Socrates's philosophy and teachings.

In the middle period, Plato now writes in his own voice on his core beliefs and ideals of justice, courage, wisdom and moderation, both of the individual and society. His most famous work, The Republic was written during this time and is a seminal work on the exploration of a just government ruled by philosopher kings.

In the late, period, Socrates is now relegated to a minor role and Plato now returns to take a closer look at his own early metaphysical ideas. The roles of art, including dance, music, drama and architecture, as well as ethics and morality are explored and expounded upon. In his writings on the Theory of Forms, Plato suggests that the world of ideas is the only consistent force and that the world we experience through our senses is deceptive.

Having now returned to Athens Plato embarked upon an extraordinary undertaking. In around 385 B.C.E., he established a school of learning, known as the Academy. Plato would preside over its teachings until his death.

The Academy's extensive curriculum included astronomy, biology, mathematics, political theory and philosophy. Plato hoped that those who studied there would be future leaders who would be better equipped thorough its teachings to understand how to build a better government in the Greek city-states.

The Academy would continue to teach and research for centuries until it was closed in 529 C.E., by the Roman Emperor Justinian I, who feared it was a source of paganism and a threat to Christianity.

In 367 B.C.E., Plato was invited by Dion, a friend and disciple, to be tutor to his nephew, Dionysius II, the new ruler of Syracuse in Sicily. Dion believed that Dionysius showed promise as a philosopher king; an ideal leader. Plato accepted but Dionysius fell far short of expectations and suspected Dion, and then Plato, of conspiring against him. Dion was exiled, and Plato put under "house arrest." Eventually, Plato returned to Athens and his beloved Academy. One of his more promising students there was Aristotle, who would shortly take Plato's teachings in new directions.

Plato's final years were spent at the Academy and immersed in his writing.

We now come to the final piece concerning our lack of knowledge; the exact nature of Plato's death. All accounts are confident he died in Athens around 348 B.C.E., a time when he would have been in his early 80's. Some suggest that he died while attending a wedding, while others contend he died peacefully in his sleep. As a romantic alternative he died in his sleep while a young girl played the flute nearby. No matter Plato the man had ceased to be but Plato the legend had begun.

Plato's ideas on philosophy and the nature of humanity has had an impact across all civilisations since. Whilst his areas of interest and work cover mathematics, science and nature, morals and political theory he understood that the use of mathematics in education has helped to develop a more complete understanding not just of our world but the entire universe. Additionally, his work on the use of reason to develop a fairer and more just society based on the equality of the individual has helped establish the foundation for modern liberal democracy.

Plato – A Concise Bibliography

Early
Apology (of Socrates)
Charmides
Crito
Euthyphro
Gorgias
Hippias (minor)
Hippias (major)
Ion
Laches
Lysis
Protagoras

Middle
Cratylus
Euthydemus

Meno
Parmenides
Phaedo
Phaedrus
Republic
Symposium,

Middle/Late
Theaetetus

Late
Critias
Sophist
Statesman/Politicus
Timaeus
Philebus
Laws

www.ingramcontent.com/pod-product-compliance
Lightning Source LLC
Chambersburg PA
CBHW060105050426
42448CB00011B/2629